STAIR DESIGN

daab

Introduction   4

Stairs have remained unperturbed by the passing of time. Their form is so intrinsically linked to their function that over the centuries they have hardly experienced any modifications at all. While the changing artistic styles may have altered decorative aspect, their essence has remained intact. Stairs, therefore, are a true reflection of artistic trends, of technological advances and of the values of an era.

Originally built from stone, stairs are still visible in the ruins of most ancient buildings that have survived until today, in particularly those that would majestically keep watch over the entrance to sacred places or centers of political power. Their construction took into account the same determining factors as it does today: their use and location. While it is true that technological innovation and the appearance of new materials have allowed architects to venture into audacious projects that appear to defy the law of gravity, the vast majority of stairs are marked, as in years gone by, by limits on space, time and money. Despite these limitations, stairs continue to be highly representative of the architect, who determines whether to give them center stage or just a background role in a project.

Stair Design brings together more than seventy recent projects from all over the world, which respond to highly diverse needs: from just a few steps compensating the changing level in a loft, to never-ending staircases that rise up the façade of a skyscraper. Included in each section and classified according to their public or private use are numerous examples of stairs built from the most commonly used materials; wood, metal, re-enforced concrete and glass, or a combination of these, often used to maximize the design's efficiency. As well as the wide-ranging sample of typologies and materials, *Stair Design* offers a selection of creative solutions for elements such as banisters or lighting, which are as fundamental as the steps themselves.

Auf dem Olymp der Elemente, die dem Lauf der Zeit unerschütterlich widerstehen, befinden sich die Treppen, deren Form so wesentlich mit ihrer Funktion verbunden ist. Auch wenn verschiedene Kunststile die dekorativen Elemente verändert haben, so blieb die Essenz der Treppen doch intakt. Die Treppe ist somit eine treue Widerspiegelung der künstlerischen Tendenzen, aber auch der Fortschritte der Technologie und der Werte einer Epoche.

Einst wurden sie aus Stein konstruiert, und wir finden Treppen in einem großen Teil der architektonischen Überreste des Altertums, die bis zum heutigen Tag erhalten blieben. Und vor allem in heiligen Stätten und dort, wo die politische Macht zu finden war, säumten majestätische und riesenhafte Treppen den Eingang. Auch heute noch werden die gleichen bedingenden Faktoren für die Konstruktion von Treppen berücksichtigt wie damals, der Zweck und der Standort. Auch wenn es so ist, dass technologische Innovationen und die Verwendung neuer Materialien es möglich machen, dass sich die Architekten an gewagte Projekte heranwagen, die den Gesetzen der Schwerkraft zu trotzen scheinen, wird man bei der Anlage von Treppen noch wie in der Vergangenheit durch räumliche, zeitliche und finanzielle Faktoren eingeschränkt. Trotz dieser Einschränkungen ist die Treppe weiterhin ein Element, das zeigt, wie gut ein Architekt arbeitet. Er muss entscheiden, ob er der Treppe eine Hauptrolle gewährt oder sie in eine Nebenrolle innerhalb des architektonischen Gesamtbildes zwingt.

Stair Design zeigt über siebzig neue Konstruktionen auf der ganzen Welt, die zu verschiedenen Zwecken entworfen wurden, angefangen mit ein paar Stufen bis hin zu unendlichen Treppen. Die Treppen werden nach öffentlicher oder privater Nutzung unterschieden und in jeder Sektion zeigen wir zahlreiche Beispiele für Treppen, die aus den üblichen Materialien wie Holz, Metall, Stahlbeton und Glas oder einer Kombination dieser Materialien konstruiert sind, eine Kombination, die mittlerweile üblich ist, um die Vorteile der verschiedenen Materialien zu nutzen und Nachteile auszugleichen. Zusätzlich zu den vielen Beispielen für Treppenmodelle und Materialien gibt es auch ein Kapitel, das kreativen Lösungen für Elemente wie Geländer oder Beleuchtung gewidmet ist, die so wichtig sind wie die Stufen selbst.

Dans l'olympe des éléments immuables face au temps qui passe, citons les escaliers, dont la forme, si étroitement liée à la fonction. Si les divers styles artistiques en ont davantage modifié l'aspect extérieur ornemental, son essence même reste intacte. L'escalier est, en fait, le reflet fidèle des courants artistiques, mais aussi des progrès technologiques et des valeurs d'une époque.

Originellement construits en pierre les escaliers sont encore visibles dans la majeure partie des vestiges architecturaux de l'Antiquité conservés jusqu'à nos jours : surtout ceux qui, majestueux et cyclopéens, marquaient l'entrée aux enceintes sacrées ou au siège du pouvoir politique. Leur construction était conditionnée par les mêmes facteurs que ceux qui prévalent encore aujourd'hui, à savoir l'usage et l'emplacement. Certes, les innovations technologiques et l'apparition de nouveaux matériaux ont permis aux architectes de s'aventurer dans d'audacieux projets semblant défier les lois de l'apesanteur, mais dans l'ensemble, les escaliers dépendent, hier comme aujourd'hui, de la limitation spatiale, temporelle et économique. Malgré une telle limitation, l'escalier reste un élément hautement représentatif du savoir-faire de l'architecte qui doit décider de lui accorder un rôle protagoniste ou le reléguer au second plan dans le cadre du projet architectural.

Stair Design réunit plus de soixante-dix projets récents du monde entier, qui correspondent aux besoins les plus divers, allant de quelques marches pour créer une petite différence de niveau dans un loft, jusqu'aux interminables escaliers qui escaladent la façade d'un gratte-ciel. Classés en fonction de leur usage à caractère public ou privé, les escaliers sont répartis en deux sections offrant de nombreux exemples réalisés dans les matériaux les plus utilisés : bois, métal, béton armé et verre, seuls ou associés, comme cela se fait de plus en plus pour maximaliser les avantages et minimiser les inconvénients. Outre un large éventail de typologies et matériaux, *Stair Design* offre une sélection de solutions créatives pour certains éléments –mains courantes ou éclairage– aussi essentiels que les marches elles-mêmes.

En el olimpo de los elementos que asisten imperturbables al paso del tiempo se encuentra la escalera, cuya forma va tan intrínsecamente ligada a su función que apenas ha sufrido modificaciones a lo largo de los siglos. Si bien los distintos estilos artísticos han ido alterando el aspecto decorativo, su esencia permanece intacta. Así, la escalera es un fiel reflejo de las corrientes artísticas, pero también de los avances de la tecnología y de los valores de una época.

Construidas originariamente con piedra, las escaleras son todavía visibles en buena parte de los vestigios arquitectónicos de la Antigüedad que se han conservado hasta nuestros días, sobre todo aquellas que, majestuosas y ciclópeas, solían marcar la entrada a los recintos sagrados o a las sedes de poder político. Su construcción tuvo en cuenta los mismos condicionantes que hoy en día: el uso y el emplazamiento. Es cierto que las innovaciones tecnológicas y la aparición de nuevos materiales han permitido que los arquitectos se aventuren en audaces proyectos que parecen desafiar las leyes de la gravedad, pero en la gran mayoría de los casos las escaleras están marcadas, como antaño, por limitaciones espaciales, temporales y económicas. A pesar de ello, la escalera continúa siendo un elemento altamente representativo del buen hacer del arquitecto, que debe decidir si le otorga un papel protagonista o la relega a un segundo plano en el conjunto del proyecto arquitectónico.

Stair Design reúne más de setenta proyectos recientes de todo el mundo que responden a necesidades muy diversas: desde unos pocos peldaños que salvan un pequeño desnivel en un loft hasta interminables escaleras que ascienden por la fachada de un rascacielos. Clasificadas según su uso público o privado, en cada apartado se incluyen numerosos ejemplos de escaleras construidas con los materiales más empleados, como la madera, el metal, el hormigón armado y el cristal, o con una combinación de todos ellos, como viene siendo habitual, a fin de sumar las ventajas y restar los inconvenientes. Además de la amplia muestra de tipologías y materiales, *Stair Design* ofrece una selección de soluciones creativas para elementos como las barandillas o la iluminación, tan fundamentales como los propios peldaños.

Tra il panorama degli elementi che assistono imperturbabili al passare del tempo vi sono le scale, la cui forma è strettamente legata alla loro funzione, che nei vari secoli è rimasta pressoché inalterata. Anche se i diversi stili artistici hanno modificato il loro lato più decorativo, la loro essenza rimane immutata. La scala, si considera pertanto, un riflesso non solo delle correnti artistiche ma anche degli ultimi progressi tecnologici e dei valori di una epoca.

Costruite originariamente in pietra, le scale rimangono tuttora visibili in buona parte delle vestigia architettoniche che si sono conservate fino ai nostri giorni, soprattutto quelle che, maestose e imponenti, solevano segnare l'entrata alle zone sacre o alle sedi del potere politico. La loro costruzione tenne conto di fattori condizionanti che continuano ad essere vigenti ancora oggi: l'uso e la loro collocazione. È vero che le innovazioni tecnologiche e la comparsa di nuovi materiali hanno fatto sì che gli architetti si avventurino in audaci progetti che sembrano sfidare le leggi di gravità, ma nella maggior parte dei casi le scale vengono definite, come accadeva una volta, da limiti spaziali e da fattori di tipo economico. Nonostante i suddetti limiti, o per l'appunto, come loro conseguenza, la scala continua ad essere un elemento altamente rappresentativo della qualità e maestria di un buon architetto, che deve decidere se concederle un ruolo protagonista o relegarla a un secondo piano nell'insieme del progetto architettonico.

Stair Design riunisce più di settanta progetti recenti, di tutto il mondo, e che rispondono ad esigenze molto diverse: da scale con pochi gradini che collegano i ridotti dislivelli di un loft, fino a interminabili scale che ascendono attorno alla facciata di un grattacielo. Classificate secondo il loro uso pubblico o privato, in ogni sezione si includono numerosi esempi di scale costruite con i materiali più utilizzati, come il legno, il metallo, il cemento armato e il vetro, o con una loro combinazione, come accade abitualmente al fine di ridurre gli inconvenienti e incrementare ulteriormente i vantaggi. Oltre a una vasta panoramica sulle tipologie e sui materiali, *Stair Design* offre una selezione di soluzioni creative per elementi quali le ringhiere o l'illuminazione, che rivestono un'importanza pari a quella degli stessi gradini.

PUBLIC STAIRS

A2RC | BRUSSELS
LES JARDINS DE LA COURONNE
Brussels, Belgium | 2005

ALEJANDRO BAHAMÓN, MINOS DIGENIS | BARCELONA
ALAVA 22 OFFICE
Barcelona, Spain | 2003

ATELIER VAN LIESHOUT, MVRDV | ROTTERDAM
LLOYD HOTEL MUSIC ROOM
Amsterdam, Netherlands | 2004

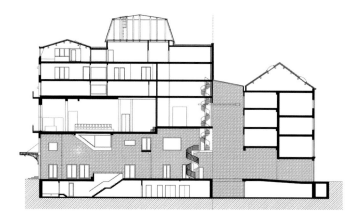

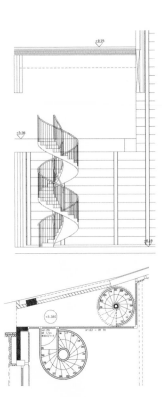

BAR ARCHITECTS | ROTTERDAM
BAK ARTS CENTER
Utrecht, Netherlands | 2003

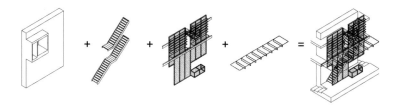

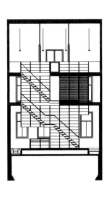

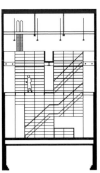

CASTEL VECIANA ARQUITECTURA | BARCELONA
AGATHA RUIZ DE LA PRADA
Madrid, Spain | 2003

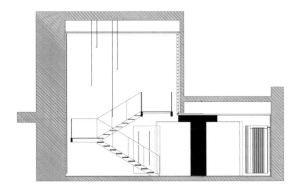

DE ARCHITEKTEN CIE | AMSTERDAM
MENZIS MAIN OFFICE
Groningen, Netherlands | 2001

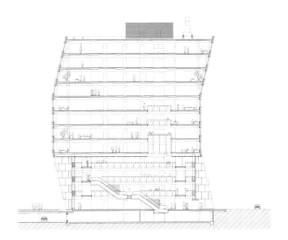

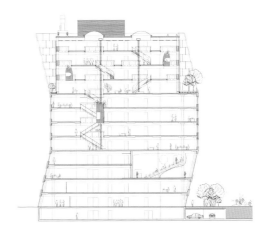

GCA ARQUITECTES | BARCELONA
AC CIUDAD DE SEVILLA HOTEL
Sevilla, Spain | 1998

GCA ARQUITECTES | BARCELONA
GONZALO COMELLA
Barcelona, Spain | 2000

GCA ARQUITECTES | BARCELONA
HOTEL CRAM
Barcelona, Spain | 2004

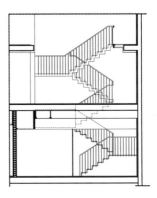

GNOSIS ARCHITETTURA | NAPLES
BPS BANK
Naples, Italy | 2003

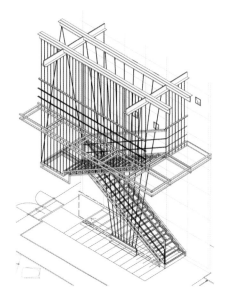

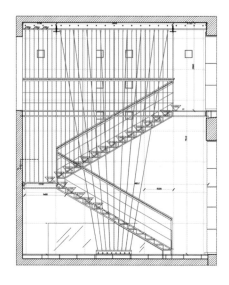

GRAY PUKSAND | SYDNEY
BENDIGO BANK
Melbourne, Australia | 2005

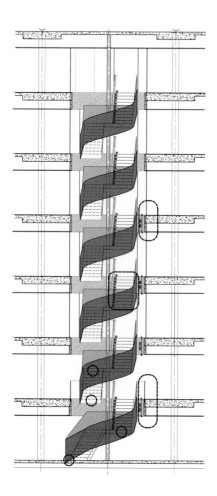

GUALTIERO OBERTI | BERGAMO
COLLEONI CASTLE RENOVATION
Solza, Italy | 2005

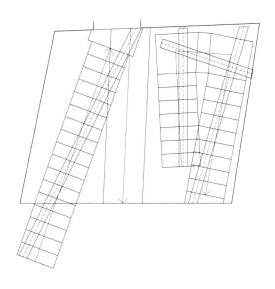

HASCHER JEHLE ARCHITEKTUR | BERLIN
STUTTGART MUSEUM OF ART
Stuttgart, Germany | 2004

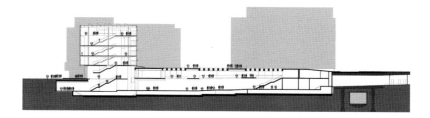

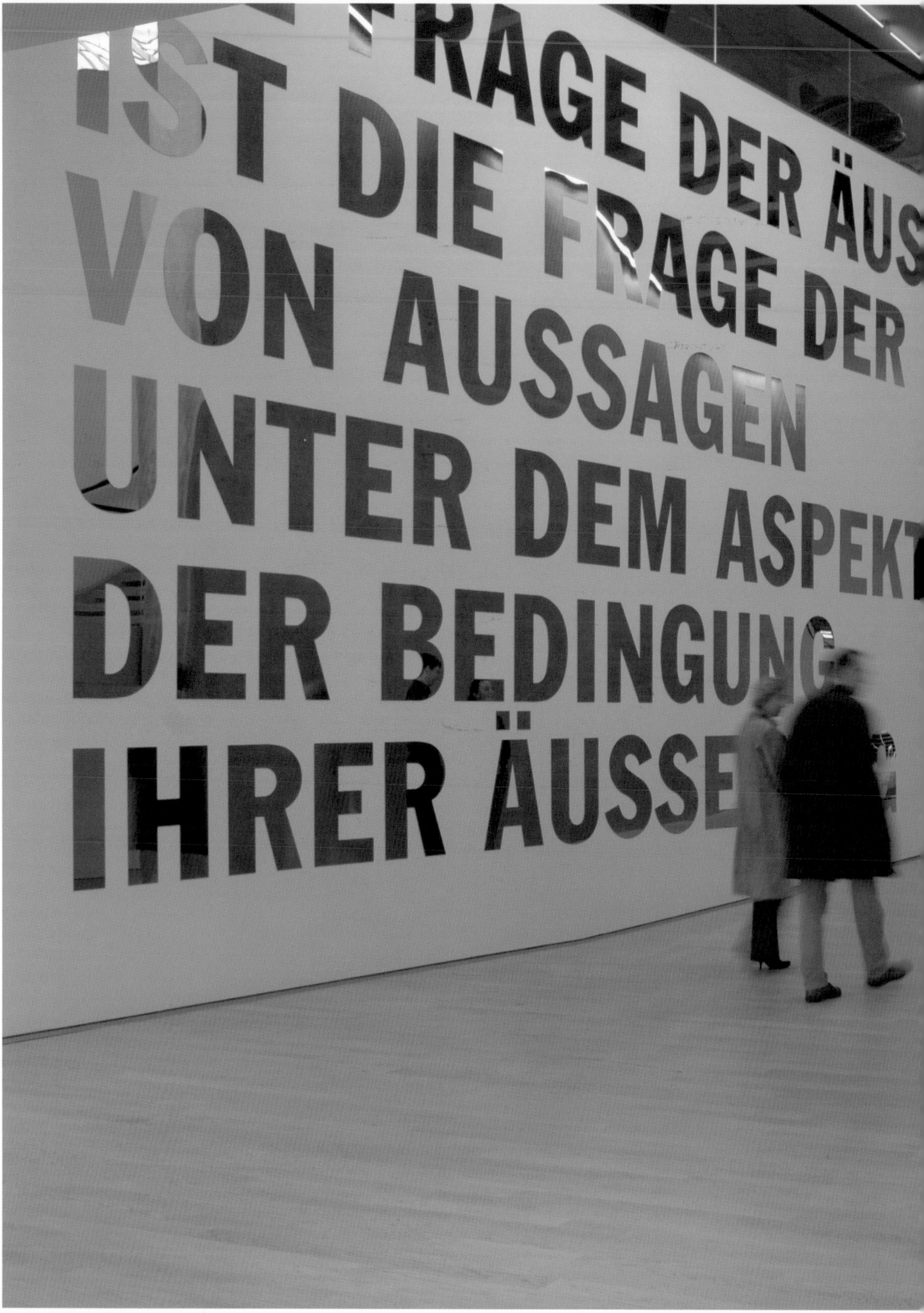

FRAGE DER ÄUS
IST DIE FRAGE DER
VON AUSSAGEN
UNTER DEM ASPEKT
DER BEDINGUNG
IHRER ÄUSSE

HERTL ARCHITEKTEN | STEYR
TECHNOLOGY HOUSE
Steyr, Austria | 2003

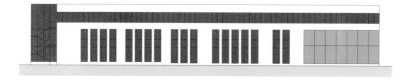

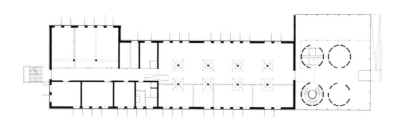

JOËL CLAISSE ARCHITECTURES | BRUSSELS
OFFICE ALLEN & OVERY
Tervuren, Belgium | 1998

JORDI MACRI | BARCELONA
ESTACIÓ DEL NORD SPORTS CENTRE
Barcelona, Spain | 1998

LLUÍS PAU | BARCELONA
LA PEDRERA MEZZANINE FLOOR RENOVATION
Barcelona, Spain | 2005

LORENZO ROSSI | FABRIANO
INDESIT HEADQUARTERS
Fabriano, Italy | 2005

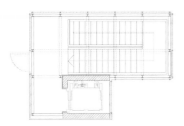

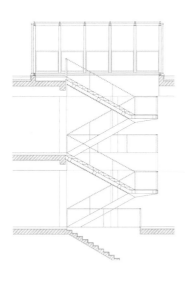

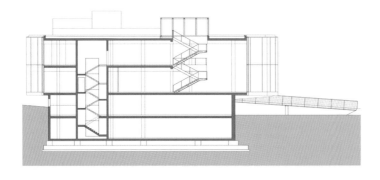

MARC PADRÓS, XAVIER VALLS | BARCELONA
COMPAK COFFEE GRINDERS HEADQUARTERS
Bigues i Riells, Spain | 2001

MOHEN DESIGN INTERNATIONAL | SHANGHAI
MOHEN DESIGN INTERNATIONAL OFFICE
Shanghai, China | 2006

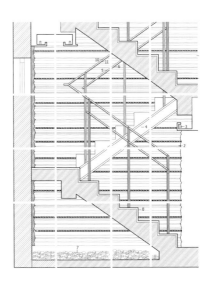

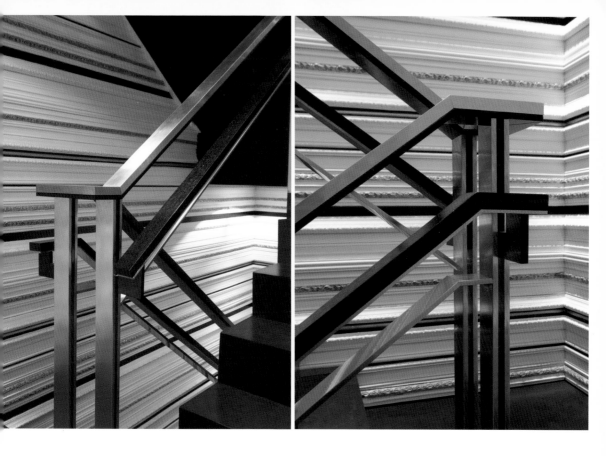

MURPHY/JAHN | CHICAGO
DEUTSCHE POST TOWER
Bonn, Germany | 2003

NOVARON | DIEPOLDSAU
FUNHOTEL THE CUBE
Tröpolach, Switzerland | 2003

OFFICE OLIVIER DWEK | BRUSSELS
OFFICE OLIVIER DWEK HEADQUARTERS
Brussels, Belgium | 2004

ONTWERPGROEP TRUDE HOOYKAAS | AMSTERDAM
TOYO ITO & ASSOCIATES | TOKYO
HOUTHOFF BURUMA BUILDING
Amsterdam, Netherlands | 2005

ÓSCAR TUSQUETS BLANCA | BARCELONA
PETIT PALAU DE LA MÚSICA
Barcelona, Spain | 2004

PAULO DAVID | FUNCHAL
CASA DAS MUDAS
Calheta, Madeira, Portugal | 2004

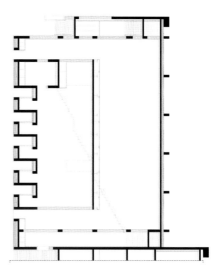

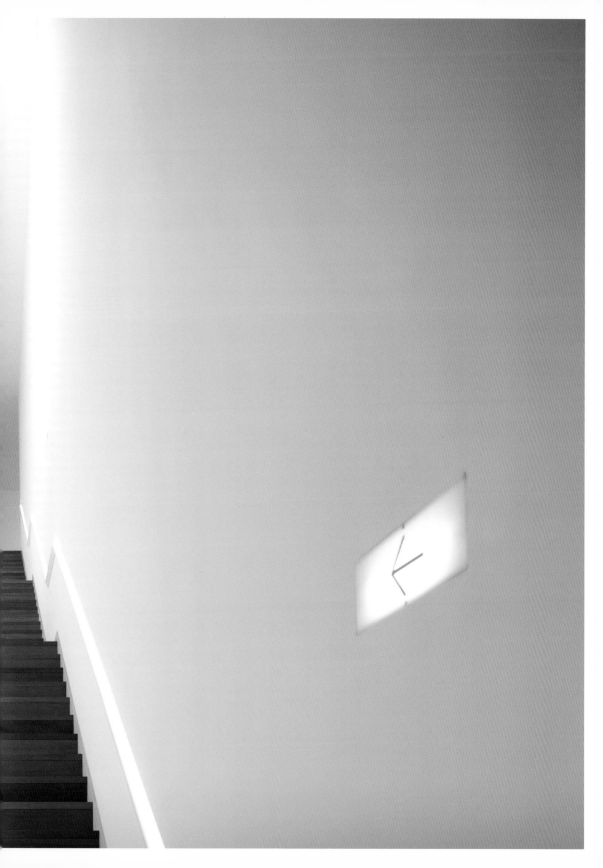

PUGH & SCARPA ARCHITECTURE | SANTA MONICA
DEKTOR HIGGINS FILM STUDIO
Hollywood, United States | 2000

PURPUR ARCHITEKTUR | GRAZ
LAPIDARIUM MUSEUM
Graz, Austria | 2004

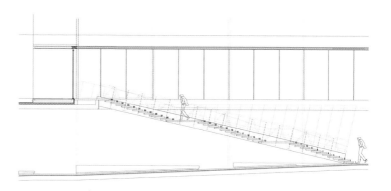

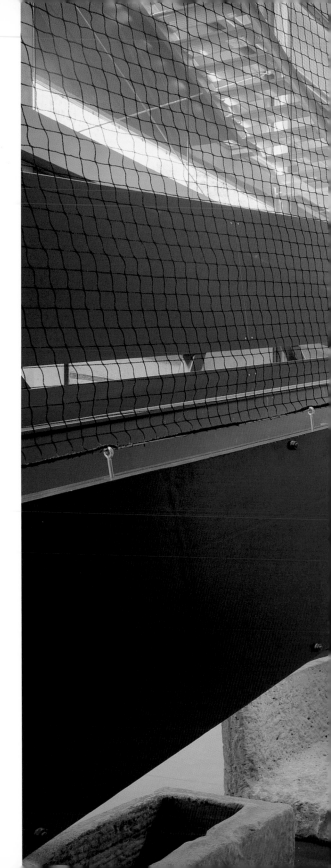

WEINE

WEISS:
PINOT GRIGIO, FLORIANI
SAUVIGNON, MARQUIS RISCH
WEISSBURGUNDER, STRBLE
WELSCHRIESLING, SATTLERH
GRÜNER VELTLINER ELDING

ROT:

PURPUR ARCHITEKTUR | GRAZ
MOCCABAR
Graz, Austria | 2003

RAFAEL VIÑOLY ARCHITECTS | NEW YORK
MAHLER 4 OFFICE TOWER
Amsterdam, Netherlands | 2005

REINER SCHMID | GRAZ
DOM IM BERG
Graz, Austria | 2000

RKW ARCHITEKTEN | DÜSSELDORF
SHOPPING MALL SEVENS
Düsseldorf, Germany | 2000

ZAHA HADID ARCHITECTS | LONDON
BMW PLANT
Leipzig, Germany | 2005

PRIVATE STAIRS

AG & F ARCHITETTI | MILAN
BW LOFT
Brescia, Italy | 2005

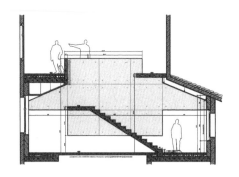

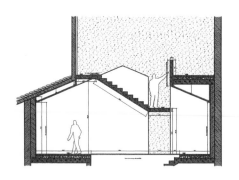

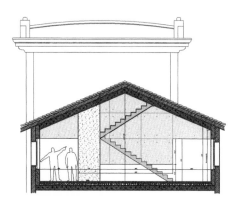

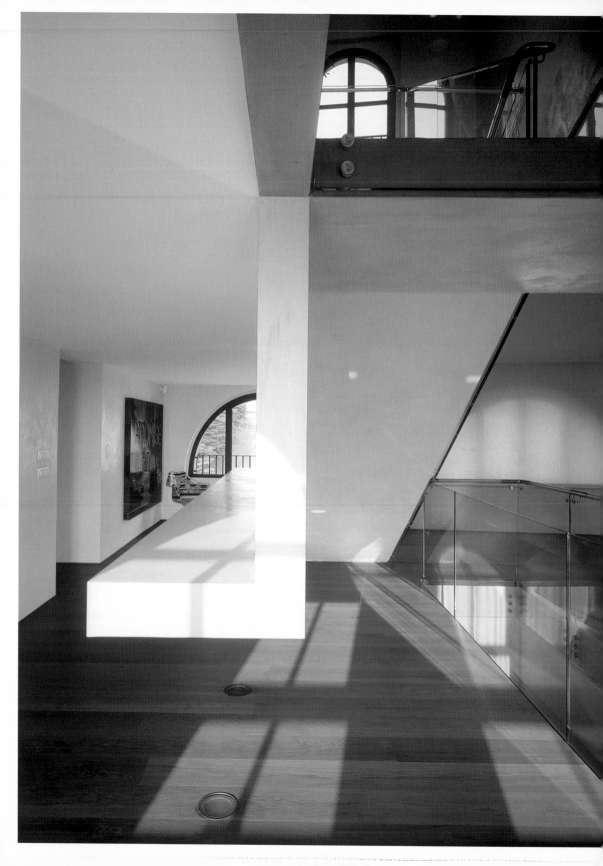

AGUSTÍ COSTA | BERGA
FLAT IN BERGA
Berga, Spain | 2004

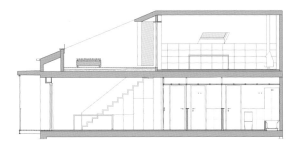

AGUSTÍ COSTA | BERGA
LOFT IN BERGA
Berga, Spain | 2004

AIDLIN DARLING DESIGN | SAN FRANCISCO
BEALE STREET LOFT
San Francisco, United States | 2002

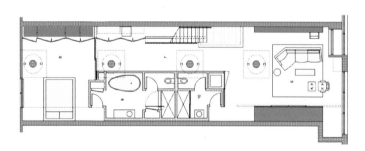

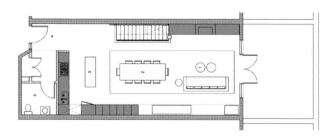

AIDLIN DARLING DESIGN | SAN FRANCISCO
VICTORIAN ROW HOUSE
San Francisco, United States | 2004

AIR PROJECTS/INÉS RODRÍGUEZ | BARCELONA
DUPLEX IN REINA VICTÒRIA
Barcelona, Spain | 2003

ALPHAVILLE/KENTARO TAKEGUCHI & ASAKO YAMAMOTO | KYOTO
WINDOW HOUSE
Tokyo, Japan | 2004

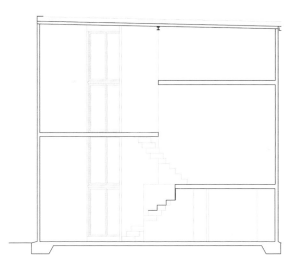

ÁLVARO LEITE SIZA VIEIRA | PORTO
HOUSE TOLÓ
Alvite, Portugal | 1999

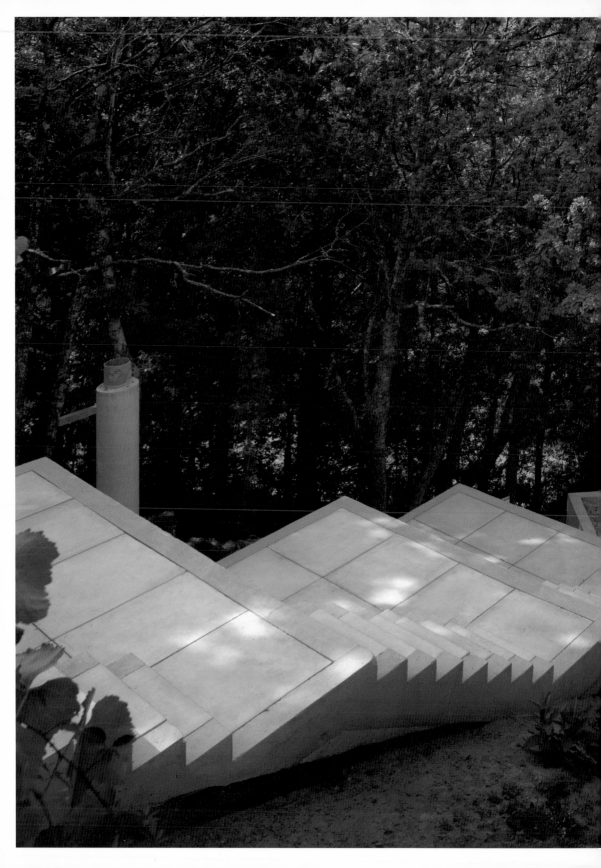

ARCHIKUBIK | BARCELONA
HOUSE H
Sant Andreu de Llavaneres, Spain | 2003

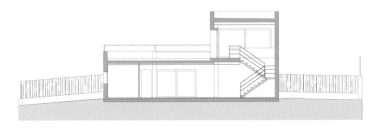

ARKAN ZEYTINOGLU | VIENNA
PENTHOUSE S
Vienna, Austria | 2005

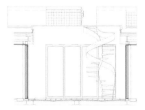

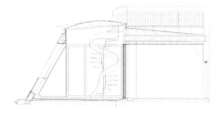

BANG – BUREAU D'ARCHITECTE NICOLAS GOUYGOU | BRUSSELS
LOFT BERTHELOT
Brussels, Belgium | 2004

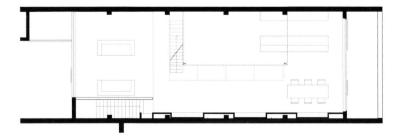

BINNBERG & EBERLE | MUNICH
HOUSE IN MUNICH
Munich, Germany | 2002

CARLOS CASTANHEIRA & CLARA BASTAI ARQUITECTOS | VILA NOVA DE GAIA
RESIDENCE IN RIBEIRA DE ABADE
Ribeira de Abade, Portugal | 2005

CHELSEA ATELIER ARCHITECT/AYHAN OZAN & CIGDEM TANIK | NEW YORK
NEW YORK DUPLEX
New York, United States | 2002

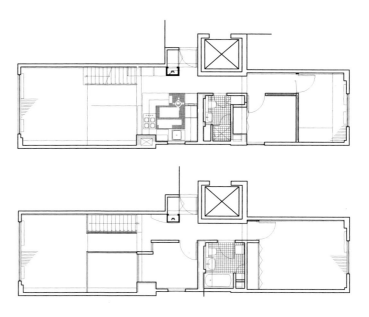

CORSIN | TARRAGONA
HOUSE IN TARRAGONA
Tarragona, Spain | 2004

CRAHAY & JAMAIGNE | MALMEDY
HABITATION MICHEL
Stavelot, Belgium | 2003

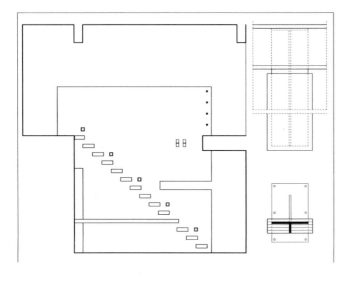

EMILIO AMBASZ & ASSOCIATES | NEW YORK
THE HOUSE OF SPIRITUAL RETREAT
Sevilla, Spain | 2004

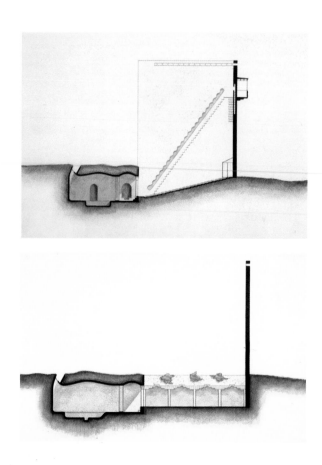

FFCB ARQUITECTOS ASSOCIADOS | LISBOA
APARTMENT IN GRANDELA
Lisboa, Portugal | 2006

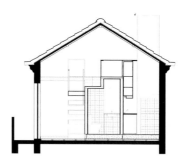

GNOSIS ARCHITETTURA | NAPLES
PERSICO HOUSE
Naples, Italy | 2003

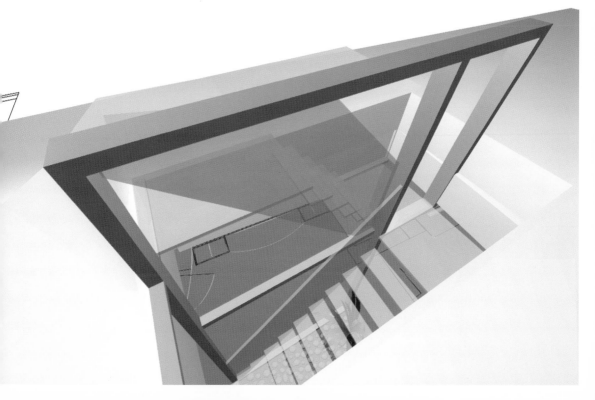

GREEK | BARCELONA
RESIDENCE IN MATADEPERA
Matadepera, Spain | 2005

HANS GANGOLY | GRAZ
HOUSE SCHMUCK 2
Graz, Austria | 2005

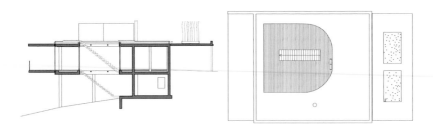

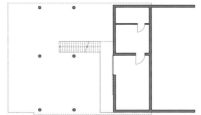

HERWIG VAN SOOM | BLANDEN
STRAW AND CLAY HOUSE
Blanden, Belgium | 2003

IRENE GRÜNDER | MUNICH
HOUSE C
Munich, Germany | 2003

JOAN BACH | BARCELONA
HOUSE IN VALLROMANES
Vallromanes, Spain | 2001

MALEK & HERBST ARCHITEKTEN | GRAZ
HOUSE B
Graz, Austria | 2005

MOJO STUMER ASSOCIATES | GREENVALE
BLAU APARTMENT
New York, United States | 2003

MOLNAR FREEMAN ARCHITECTS | WOOLLAHRA
HOUSE IN BALGOWLAH
Balgowlah, Australia | 2004

MVRDV | ROTTERDAM
FRØSILOS
Copenhagen, Denmark | 2005

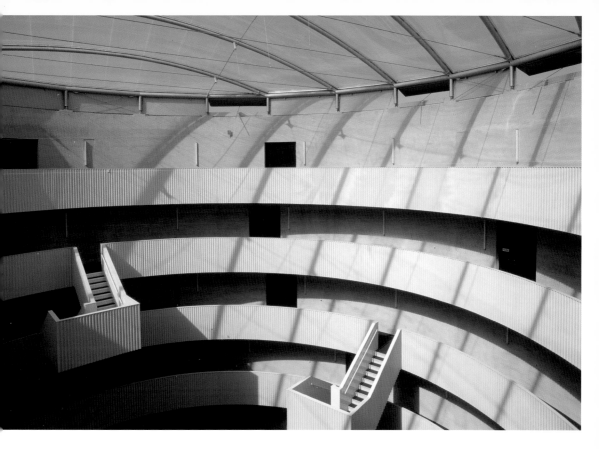

MVRDV | ROTTERDAM
MIRADOR
Madrid, Spain | 2004

NUNO BRANDÃO COSTA | PORTO
HOUSE IN AFIFE
Afife, Portugal | 2004

OFFICE OLIVIER DWEK | BRUSSELS
HOUSE ELSA
Brussels, Belgium | 2005

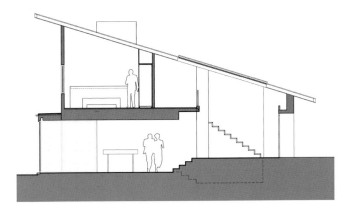

OFIS ARHITEKTI | LJUBLJANA
SLEEPING STAIRCASE
Ljubljana, Slovenia | 2002

OFIS ARHITEKTI | LJUBLJANA
VILLA BLED
Bled, Slovenia | 2003

PIDECSER/MONTSE I RAMON PIDEVALL | GARRAF
GARRAF APARTMENT
Garraf, Spain | 2003

PUGH & SCARPA ARCHITECTURE | SANTA MONICA
SOLAR UMBRELLA
Venice, United States | 2005

ROCKHILL & ASSOCIATES | LECOMPTON
PORSCH HOUSE
Lawrence, United States | 2000

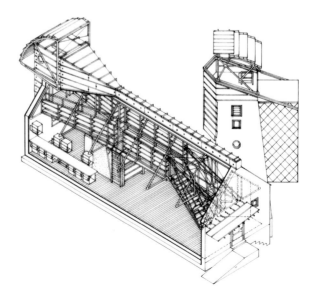

SCHELLEN ARCHITECTS | BONHEIDEN
RESIDENCE IN ENGHIEN
Enghien, Brussels | 1998

SETH STEIN ARCHITECTS | LONDON
HOUSE IN VICENZA
Vicenza, Italy | 2005

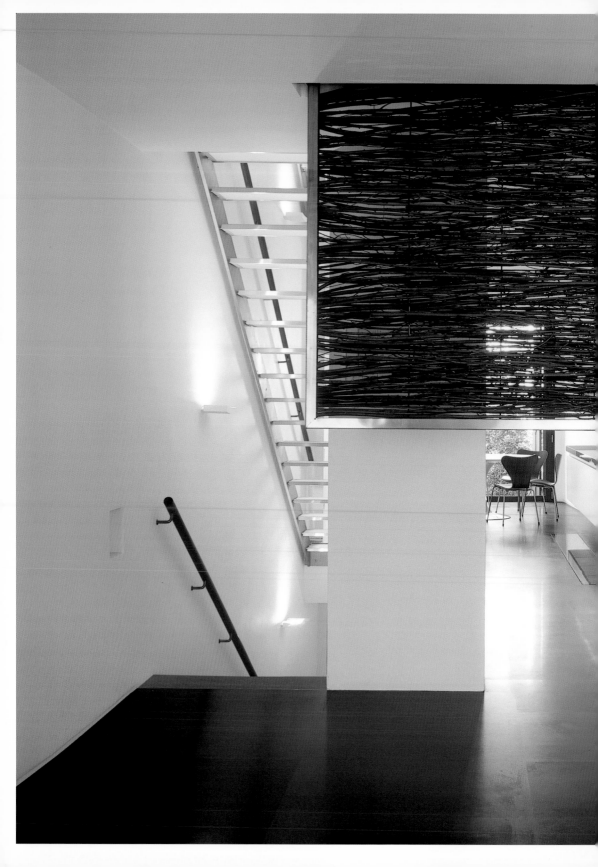

STUDIJA LAPE | VILNIUS
RESIDENCE IN VILNIUS
Vilnius, Lithuania | 2005

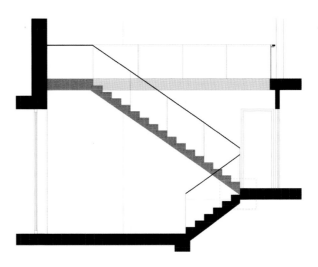

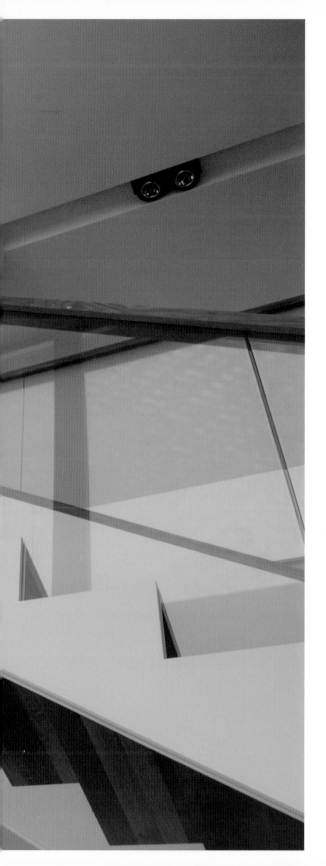

TOW STUDIOS ARCHITECTURE | NEW YORK
APARTMENT IN GREENWICH VILLAGE
New York, United States | 2005

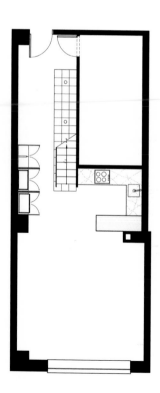

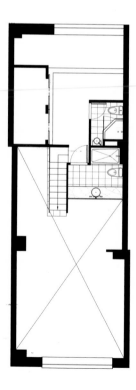

UBALDO GARCÍA TORRENTE | SEVILLA
CASTLE HOUSE
Sevilla, Spain | 2005

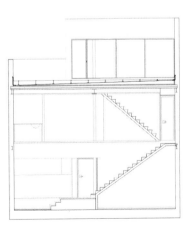

A2RC
27, Galerie du Roi
B-1000 Brussels, Belgium
P +32 02 511 47 09
F +32 02 511 23 36
a2rc@a2rc.be
www.a2rc.be
Les jardins de la Couronne
Photos: © Laurent Brandajs

AG & F Architetti
Via G. C. Procaccini 47
20154 Milan, Italy
P +39 023 453 8625
F +39 023 493 5321
agf@architetti.fastwebnet.it
BW Loft
Photos: © Andrea Martiradonna

Agustí Costa
Plaça de la Creu, 3, 2.º 2.ª
08600 Berga, Spain
P +34 938 211 063
F +34 938 221 105
estudi@agusticosta.com
www.agusticosta.com
Flat in Berga
Loft in Berga
Photos: © David Cardelús

Aidlin Darling Design
500 Third Street, Suite 410
San Francisco, CA 94107, USA
P +1 415 974 5603
F +1 415 974 0849
info@aidlin-darling-design.com
www.aidlin-darling-design.com
Beale Street Loft
Victorian Row House
Photos: © John Sutton

Air Projects/Inés Rodríguez
Pau Claris, 179, 3.º 1.ª
08037 Barcelona, Spain
P +34 932 722 427
F +34 932 722 428
info@air-projects.com
www.air-projects.com
Duplex in Reina Victòria
Photos: © Jordi Miralles

Alejandro Bahamón
Rec, 60, pral. 1.ª
08003 Barcelona, Spain
P +34 933 151 661
alejandrobahamon@telefonica.net
Alava 22 Office
Photos: © Stephan Ach

Alphaville/Kentaro Takeguchi & Asako Yamamoto
32 Kamihanada-cho, Saiin Ukyo-ku
615-0007 Kyoto, Japan
P +81 75 312 6951
F +81 75 312 0416
alphavil@a1.ethink.jp
www.a1.ethink.jp/~alphavil
Window House
Photos: © Kei Sugino

Álvaro Leite Siza Vieira
Rua Do Aleixo 53, C/A
4450-043 Porto, Portugal
P +351 226 108 575
F +351 226 108 574
House Toló
Photos: © FG+SG/Fernando Guerra

Archikubik
Lluís Antúnez, 6
08006 Barcelona, Spain
P +34 934 152 762
info@archikubik.com
www.archikubik.com
House H
Photos: © Miquel Tres

Arkan Zeytinoglu
Mariahilfer Strasse 101/3/51
A-1060 Vienna, Austria
P +43 1 595 38 04
F +43 1 595 38 04 16
office@arkan.at
www.arkan.at
Penthouse S
Photos: © Angelo Kaunat

Atelier Van Lieshout
Keilestraat 43e
3029 BP Rotterdam, Netherlands
P +31 10 244 09 71
F +31 10 244 09 72
info@ateliervanlieshout.com
www.ateliervanlieshout.com
Lloyd Hotel Music Room
Photos: © Rob't Hart

B-Architecten
Borgerhoutsestraat 22/01
2018 Antwerpen, Belgium
P +32 (0)3 231 82 28
F +32 (0)3 231 92 49
info@b-architecten.be
www.b-architecten.be
The Beurschouwburg
Photos: © Laurent Brandajs

BANG–Bureau d'Architecte Nicolas Gouygou
Rue Egide Van Ophem 108
1180 Brussels, Belgium
P +32 02 370 46 50
F +32 02 370 46 92
bang@skynet.be
Loft Berthelot
Photos: © Laurent Brandajs

Bar Architects
Pelgrimstraat 5-B
NL 3029 BH Rotterdam, Netherlands
P +31 10 477 38 63
F +31 10 476 66 15
info@bararchitects.com
www.bararchitects.com
Bak Arts Center
Photos: © Rob't Hart

Binnberg & Eberle
Steinstrasse 28
81667 Munich, Germany
P +49 089 4808 8630
F +49 089 4808 8650
info@binnberg-eberle.de
www.binnberg-eberle.de
House in Munich
Photos: © Angelo Kaunat

Carlos Castanheira & Clara Bastai Arquitectos
Rua Conselheiro Veloso da Cruz, 61
4400-094 Vila Nova de Gaia, Portugal
P +351 223 704 710
F +351 223 704 098
castanheira.arqtos@net.novis.pt
Residence in Ribeira de Abade
Photos: © FG+SG/Fernando Guerra

Castel Veciana Arquitectura
Pamplona, 88
08018 Barcelona, Spain
P +34 933 568 818
F +34 933 568 817
veciana@castelveciana.com
www.castelveciana.com
Agatha Ruiz de la Prada
Photos: © Thomas Mayer

Chelsea Atelier Architect/Ayhan Ozan & Cigdem Tanik
245 7th Avenue, Suite 6A
New York, NY 10001, USA
P +1 212 255 3494
F +1 212 255 3495
info@chelseaatelier.com
www.chelseaatelier.com
New York Duplex
Photos: © Bjorg Magnea

Corsin
Passeig de L'Esquirol, 10
43008 Tarragona, Spain
P/F +34 977 658 065
corsin@gmail.com
House in Tarragona
Photos: © Jordi Miralles

Crahay & Jamaigne
Rue de la Tannerie 1
B-4960 Malmedy, Belgium
P +32 08 067 22 03
F +32 08 067 22 05
architectes@crahayjamaigne.com
www.crahayjamaigne.com
Habitation Michel
Photos: © Laurent Brandajs

De Architekten Cie
Postbus 576
NL-1000 AN Amsterdam, Netherlands
P +31 020 5309 300/387
F +31 020 5309 399
arch@cie.nl
www.cie.nl
Menzis Main Office
Photos: © Luuk Kramer

Emilio Ambasz & Associates
8 East 62 Street
New York, NY 10021, USA
P +1 212 751 3517
F +1 212 751 0294
info@ambasz.com
www.ambasz.com
The House of Spiritual Retreat
Photos: © Fernando Alda

FFCB Arquitectos Associados
Rua do Cruzeiro, 130 A
1300-171 Lisboa, Portugal
P +351 21 362 37 37
F +351 21 362 37 36
atelier@ffcb.pt
www.ffcb.pt
Apartment in Grandela
Photos: © FG+SG/Fernando Guerra

GCA Arquitectes Associats
València, 289
08009 Barcelona, Spain
P +34 934 761 800
F +34 934 761 806
info@gcaarq.com
www.gcaarq.com
AC Ciudad de Sevilla Hotel
Gonzalo Comella
Hotel Cram
Photos: © Jordi Miralles

Gnosis Architettura
368 Via Toledo
80132 Naples, Italy
P +39 081 552 33 12
F +39 081 552 25 58
gnosis@gnosisarchitettura.it
www.gnosisarchitettura.it
BPS Bank
Persico House
Photos: © Gnosis Architettura

Gray Puksand
Level 5, 8 Spring Street
Sydney, NSW 2000, Australia
P +61 02 9247 9422
F +61 02 9247 9433
sydney@graypuksand.com.au
www.graypuksand.com.au
Bendigo Bank
Photos: © Shania Shegedyn

Greek
Rubinstein, 4
08022 Barcelona, Spain
P +34 934 189 550
F +34 934 189 532
greek@greekbcn.com
www.greekbcn.com
Residence in Matadepera
Photos: © Núria Fuentes

Gualtiero Oberti
Via degli Assonica 3
Sorisole, Bergamo, Italy
P/F +39 035 573 120
gualtiero.oberti@awn.it
Colleoni Castle Renovation
Photos: © Andrea Martiradonna

Hans Gangoly
Volksgartenstrasse 18
A-8020 Graz, Austria
P +43 316 71 75 50 0
F +43 316 71 75 50 6
office@gangoly.at
www.gangoly.at
House Schmuck 2
Photos: © Paul Ott

Hascher Jehle Architektur
Otto-Suhr-Allee 59
D-10585 Berlin, Germany
P +49 30 34 79 76 50
F +49 30 34 79 76 55
info@hascherjehle.de
www.hascher-jehle.de
Stuttgart Museum of Art
Photos: © Thomas Mayer

Hertl Architekten
Zwischenbrücken 4
4400 Steyr, Austria
P +43 7252 46944
F +43 7252 47363
steyr@hertl-architekten.com
www.hertl-architekten.com
Technology House
Photos: © Paul Ott

Herwig Van Soom
Kouterstraat 7
3052 Blanden, Belgium
P +32 16 403 517
F +32 16 230 292
orcaherwig@skynet.be
www.nebraskabe.tk
Straw and Clay House
Photos: © Laurent Brandajs

Irene Gründer
Munich, Germany
P +49 700 4783 6337
House C
Photos: © Angelo Kaunat

Joan Bach
Passeig de Gràcia, 52, pral.
08007 Barcelona, Spain
P +34 934 881 925
F +34 934 871 640
House in Vallromanes
Photos: © Jordi Miralles

Joël Claisse Architectures
Avenue Wielemans Ceuppens, 45, bte. 2
1190 Brussels, Belgium
P +32 02 346 13 26
F +32 02 346 13 19
contact@claisse-architecte.be
www.claisse-architecte.be
Office Allen & Overy
Photos: © Laurent Brandajs

Jordi Macri
Gran Via de les Corts Catalanes, 839, 3.º 3ª, esc. B
08018 Barcelona, Spain
P +34 933 569 979
macri@coac.es
Estació del Nord Sports Centre
Photos: © Jordi Miralles

Lluís Pau
Plaça Reial, 18, 2.º 1.ª
08002 Barcelona, Spain
P +34 933 176 012
F +34 933 177 266
lluispau@mbmarquitectes.com
www.mbmarquitectes.com
La Pedrera Mezzanine Floor Renovation
Photos: © Rafael Vargas

Lorenzo Rossi
Via Bocci 22,
60044 Fabriano, Italy
P +39 333 3886562
F +39 0732 627350
info@lorenzorossi.it
www.lorenzorossi.it
Indesit Headquarters
Photos: © Andrea Martiradonna

Malek & Herbst Architekten
Körösistrasse 17
A-8010 Graz, Austria
P +43 0316 681 440-0
F +43 0316 681 440-33
office@arch-malek.com
www.arch-malek.com
House B
Photos: © Angelo Kaunat

Marc Padrós
Passeig Picasso, 14, esc. 2
08003 Barcelona, Spain
P +34 933 105 344
F +34 933 105 344
marc@coac.net
Compak Coffee Grinders Headquarters
Photos: © Jordi Miralles

Minos Digenis
Pallars, 160 bis, local 6
Barcelona 08005, Spain
P +34 933 208 050
160bis@coac.net
Alava 22 Office
Photos: © Stephan Ach

Mohen Design International
No. 18 Alley 396, Wulumuqi S. Road
200031 Shanghai, China
P +86 21 6437 0910
F +86 21 6431 7125
mohen@mohen-design.com
www.mohen-design.com
Mohen Design International Office
Photos: © MoHen Design International

Mojo Stumer Associates
14 Plaza Road
Greenvale, NY 11548, USA
P + 1 516 625 3344
F + 1 516 625 3418
web@mojostumer.com
www.mojostumer.com
Blau Apartment
Photos: © Mojo Stumer Associates

Molnar Freeman Architects
14 Moncur St
Woollahra, NSW 2025, Australia
P +61 02 9327 1926
F +61 02 9327 1946
mfa@molnarfreeman.com
www.molnarfreeman.com
House in Balgowlah
Photos: © Murray Fredericks

Murphy/Jahn
35 East Wacker Drive, 3rd floor
Chicago, IL 60601, USA
P + 1 312 427 7300
F + 1 312 332 0274
info@murphyjahn.com
www.murphyjahn.com
Deutsche Post Tower
Photos: © Thomas Mayer

MVRDV
Dunantstraat 10
3024 BC Rotterdam, Netherlands
P +31 10 477 28 60
F +31 10 477 36 27
office@mvrdv.nl
www.mvrdv.nl
Lloyd Hotel Music Room
Frøsilos
Mirador
Photos: © Rob't Hart

Novaron
Sonnenstrasse 12
CH-9444 Diepoldsau, Switzerland
P +41 071 737 71 61
F +41 071 737 71 60
novaron@novaron.ch
www.novaron.ch
Funhotel The Cube
Photos: © Angelo Kaunat

Nuno Brandão Costa
Rua da Boavista 342, C27
4050-102 Porto, Portugal
P/F +351 22 203 32 17
nunobc@tvtel.pt
House in Afife
Photos: © FG+SG/Fernando Guerra

Office Olivier Dwek
34 Avenue Brugmann
1060 Brussels, Belgium
P +32 2 344 28 04
F +32 2 344 28 00
dwek.architectes@gmail.com
Office Olivier Dwek Headquarters
House Elsa
Photos: © Laurent Brandajs

Ofis Arhitekti
Kongresni Trg 3
1000 Ljubljana, Slovenia
P +386 1 426 00 85/426 00 84
F +386 1 426 00 85
ofis@ofis-a.si
www.ofis-a.si
Sleeping Staircase
Villa Bled
Photos: © Tomaz Gregoric

Ontwerpgroep Trude Hooykaas
Kruithuisstraat 23
1018 WJ Amsterdam, Netherlands
P +31 020 627 45 78
F +31 020 627 36 49
info@oth.nl
www.oth.nl
Houthoff Buruma Building
Photos: © Luuk Kramer

Óscar Tusquets Blanca
Cavallers, 50
08034 Barcelona, Spain
P +34 932 065 580
F +34 932 804 071
info@tusquets.com
www.tusquets.com
Petit Palau de la Música
Photos: © Rafael Vargas

Paulo David
Rua da Carreira 73, 5º
9000 042 Funchal, Madeira, Portugal
P +351 291 28 18 40
F +351 291 28 18 52
pd.arq@mail.telepac.pt
Casa das Mudas
Photos: © FG+SG/Fernando Guerra

Pidecser/Montse i Ramon Pidevall
Plaça Baró de Güell, 5
08871 Garraf, Spain
P +34 639 317 152
pidecsersl@teleline.es
Garraf Apartment
Photos: © Núria Fuentes

Pugh & Scarpa Architecture
2525 Michigan Ave. Building F1
Santa Monica, CA 90404, USA
P +1 310 828 0226
F +1 310 453 9609
info@pugh-scarpa.com
www.pugh-scarpa.com
Solar Umbrella
Dektor Higgins Film Studio
Photos: © Pugh & Scarpa Architecture

Purpur Architektur
Brockmanngasse 5
8010 Graz, Austria
P +43 0316 837323 0
F +43 0316 837323 83
studio@purpur.cc
www.purpur.cc
Lapidarium Museum
Moccabar
Photos: © Angelo Kaunat

Rafael Viñoly Architects
50 Vandam Street,
New York, NY 10013, USA
P + 1 212 924 5060
F + 1 212 924 5858
info@rvapc.com
www.rvapc.com
Mahler 4 Office Tower
Photos: © Luuk Kramer

Reiner Schmid
Graz, Austria
P + 43 316 833 688
rmsarch@magnet.at
Dom im Berg
Photos: © Angelo Kaunat

RKW Architekten
Tersteegenstraße 30
D-40474 Düsseldorf, Germany
P + 49 0211 43 67 0
F + 49 0211 43 67 111
info@rkwmail.de
www.rkw-as.de
Shopping Mall Sevens
Photos: © Thomas Mayer

Rockhill & Associates
1546 E350 Lecompton
Kansas, USA
P + 1 785 393 0747
F + 1 785 887 3936
rockhill@kans.com
www.rockhillandassociates.com
Porsch House
Photos: © Rockhill and Associates

Schellen Architects
Boslaan 26
2820 Bonheiden, Belgium
P + 32 015 42 05 25
F + 32 015 43 31 37
reginald.schellen@pandora.be
www.schellen.be
Residence in Enghien
Photos: © Laurent Brandajs

Seth Stein Architects
15 Grand Union Centre, West Row, Ladbroke Grove
W10 5AS London, UK
P + 44 0 20 8968 8581
F + 44 0 20 8968 8591
admin@sethstein.com
www.sethstein.com
House in Vicenza
Photos: © Andrea Martiradonna

Studija Lape
Gedimino pr. 28/2-708
2006 Vilnius, Lithuania
P + 370 5 2610809
studija@lape.lt
www.lape.lt
Residence in Vilnius
Photos: © Studija Lape

Tow Studios Architecture
131 Varick Street 1033
New York, NY 10013, USA
P + 1 646 638 4760
F + 1 646 638 4761
pt@towarchitecture.com
www.towarchitecture.com
Apartment in Greenwich Village
Photos: © Bjorg Magnea

Toyo Ito & Associates Architects
Fujiya Bldg. 19-4, 1-Chome, Shibuya, Shibuya-ku
Tokyo, 150-0002, Japan
P + 81 3 3409 5822
F + 81 3 3409 5969
www.toyo-ito.co.jp
Houthoff Buruma Building
Photos: © Luuk Kramer

Ubaldo García Torrente
Siete Revueltas, 7
41004 Sevilla, Spain
P + 34 954 229 932
7R7@telefonica.net
Castle House
Photos: © Fernando Alda

Xavier Valls
Passeig Picasso, 14, entr. 2.ª
08003 Barcelona, Spain
P + 34 933 105 344
F + 34 933 105 344
xvalls@coac.net
Compak Coffee Grinders Headquarters
Photos: © Jordi Miralles

Zaha Hadid Architects
Studio 9, 10 Bowling Green Lane
EC1R 0Q London, UK
P + 44 (0) 20 7253 5147
F + 44 (0) 20 7251 8322
mail@zaha-hadid.com
www.zaha-hadid.com
BWM Plant
Photos: © Thomas Mayer

© 2006 daab
cologne london new york

published and distributed worldwide by
daab gmbh
friesenstr. 50
d - 50670 köln

p + 49 - 221 - 913 927 0
f + 49 - 221 - 913 927 20

mail@daab-online.com
www.daab-online.com

publisher ralf daab
rdaab@daab-online.com

creative director feyyaz
mail@feyyaz.com

editorial project by loft publications
© 2006 loft publications

editor and text àgata losantos

layout zahira rodríguez mediavilla
english translation jay noden
french translation marion westerhoff
italian translation maurizio siliato
german translation susanne engler
copy editing cristina doncel

printed in spain
anman gràfiques del vallès, spain
www.anman.com

isbn-10   3-937718-64-8
isbn-13   978-3-937718-64-4
dl   B-43641-06